Objects and Plan

OF AN

INSTITUTE OF TECHNOLOGY;

INCLUDING

A SOCIETY OF ARTS, A MUSEUM OF ARTS, AND A SCHOOL OF INDUSTRIAL SCIENCE.

PROPOSED TO BE ESTABLISHED IN BOSTON.

Prepared by Direction of the Committee of Associated Institutions of Science and Arts

AND ADDRESSED TO

MANUFACTURERS, MERCHANTS, MECHANICS, AGRICULTURISTS, AND OTHER FRIENDS OF ENLIGHTENED INDUSTRY IN THE COMMONWEALTH.

Second Edition.

BOSTON:
PRINTED BY JOHN WILSON AND SON,
22, School Street.

1861.

Objects and Plan

OF AN

INSTITUTE OF TECHNOLOGY;

INCLUDING

A SOCIETY OF ARTS, A MUSEUM OF ARTS, AND A SCHOOL OF INDUSTRIAL SCIENCE.

PROPOSED TO BE ESTABLISHED IN BOSTON.

Prepared by Direction of the Committee of Associated Institutions of Science and Arts;

AND ADDRESSED TO

MANUFACTURERS, MERCHANTS, MECHANICS, AGRICULTURISTS, AND OTHER FRIENDS OF ENLIGHTENED INDUSTRY IN THE COMMONWEALTH.

Second Edition.

BOSTON:
PRINTED BY JOHN WILSON AND SON,
22, SCHOOL STREET.
1861.

INSTITUTE OF TECHNOLOGY.

In submitting to our fellow-citizens the following outline of an Institute of Technology, to be established, if practicable, on the Back-Bay lands in Boston, the undersigned are desirous of enlisting the sympathy, and securing the aid and counsel, of the friends of Industrial Art and of General Education throughout the Commonwealth.

We believe that the great practical value of the results at which we aim, although freely admitted by the friends of genuine progress everywhere, must be recognized with especial heartiness in a community like our own, where material prosperity and intellectual advancement are felt to be inseparably associated; and we feel assured that the magnitude of the plans by which it is proposed to secure these great public benefits, instead of forming an obstacle to their attainment, will but invite our fellow-citizens to a liberality proportioned to the interests to be subserved.

In the recent progress of the Industrial Arts, — including commerce and agriculture, as well as the manufacturing, and, more strictly, mechanical pursuits, — we meet with daily-increasing proofs of the happy influence of scientific culture on the industry and the civilization of nations. The Arts, no longer confining themselves to a mere empirical routine, seek to refer their processes to scientific laws, and, in many departments, justly claim the dignity of applied science. The practical nature of the discoveries in chemistry, mechanics, geology, and other branches of scientific inquiry, has multiplied almost infinitely the lines of connection between them and the processes of the Workshop, the Manufactory, and the Farm, and of the Constructive and Locomotive Arts; and these countless connecting threads, woven into one indissoluble texture, form that ever-enlarging web which is the blended product of the world's scientific and industrial activity.

In view of this recognized connection between industrial progress and an enlarged acquaintance with the objects and phenomena of nature and with physical laws, we find that the most enlightened communities of Europe have endeavored to provide for the practical co-operation of Education and the Arts, by the establishment of Museums, Societies, and Colleges of Technology. Of the great benefits which these organizations have conferred, and continue to bestow, upon the various practical Arts and upon popular education, we are assured by the records of their progress, and yet more by the lively desire so generally manifest to augment their number and extend their means of usefulness. The history of the Conservatoire des Arts and the École Centrale of Paris, and of the Kensington Museum, the School of Mines, the Museums of Economic Geology and Botany, and other like but less conspicuous institutions on the Continent and in Great Britain, has been such, both as regards the progress of the Arts and the diffusion of practical knowledge, as may well incite the friends of enlightened industry in this country to systematic efforts in the same direction.

In New England, and especially in our own Commonwealth, the time has arrived when, as we believe, the interests of Commerce and the Arts, as well as of General Education, call for the most earnest co-operation of intelligent culture with industrial pursuits. Our success hitherto in the competitions of trade, manufactures, and the other productive Arts, has been the admitted result of the superior intelligence which has inspired our enterprise and guided our activity; but, to secure a steady prosperity in the midst of the busy inventions and rapidly expanding knowledge which mark these pursuits in the leading European nations, we feel that it has become indispensable for us to provide, at least as effectually as they have done, such facilities for practical knowledge, and for the intelligent guidance of enterprise and labor, as may make our progress commensurate, step by step, with the advances of scientific and practical discovery.

While the vast and increasing magnitude of the industrial interests of New England furnishes a powerful incentive to the establishment within its borders of an Institution devoted to technological uses, it cannot be doubted that the concentration of these interests in so great a degree, in and around Boston, renders the capital of the State an eligible site for such an undertaking. Indeed, considering the peculiar genius of our busy population for the Practical Arts, and marking their avidity in the study of scientific facts and principles tending to explain or advance them, we see a special and most striking fitness in the establishment of such an Institution among them, and we gather a confident assurance of its pre-eminent utility and success. Nor can we advert to the intelligence which is so well known as guiding the large munificence of our community, without taking encouragement in the inception of the enterprise, and feeling the assurance, that whatever is adapted to advance the industrial and educational interests of the Commonwealth will receive from them the heartiest sympathy and support.

With the view of securing the great industrial and educational benefits above alluded to, it is proposed to establish, on a comprehensive plan, an Institution devoted to the Practical Arts and Sciences, to be called the MASSACHUSETTS INSTITUTE OF TECHNOLOGY, having the triple organization of a Society of Arts, a Museum or Conservatory of Arts, and a School of Industrial Science and Art.

I. SOCIETY OF ARTS OF THE INSTITUTE.

Under the first of these characters, — that of a Society of Arts, — the Institute of Technology would form itself into a department of investigation and publication, intended to promote research in connection with industrial science, by the exhibition, at the meetings of the Society, of new mechanical inventions, products, and processes; by written and oral communications and discussions, as well as by more elaborate treatises on special subjects of inquiry; and by the preparation and publication, statedly, of Reports exhibiting the condition of the various departments of industry, the progress of practical discovery in each, and the bearings of the scientific and other questions which are found to be associated with their advancement.

In this connection, we would hope to secure, as an important feature of our plan, the establishment of a *Journal of Industrial Science and Art*, which, besides setting forth the proceedings of the Society, and the condition and progress of the Museum and School of Industrial Science, should furnish a faithful record of the advance of the Arts and Practical Sciences at home and abroad.

A journal devoted to these objects, judiciously and ably conducted, would, we are confident, prove an invaluable help in carrying forward the plans and promoting the success of the Institute; and would, at the same time, form one of the most powerful means for advancing the interests of the industrial Arts and Practical Education throughout our country. Hitherto, in the United States, we have had no periodical occupying so large a field of the Applied Sciences as is here contemplated; and we cannot doubt that such a publication would be warmly welcomed by those who are professionally or otherwise interested in these pursuits.

It does not seem necessary at present to enter into the details of organization which may be deemed expedient in the operations of the Institute, in its character of a Society of Arts. These would be framed for the most part, especially as regards its government and its business relations, with a reference to the arrangements which similar societies elsewhere have found to be the simplest and most effective. Its general regulation would, as usual, devolve on a President, two or more Vice-Presidents, a Council, Secretary, and other necessary executive and financial officers, to be appointed in such form, and for such times, as might hereafter be deemed advisable. The effective operations of the Institute would, however, we think, mainly depend upon the Committees, Curators, and Professors appointed to the charge of its various departments.

As of leading importance among these Committees, we would suggest the following, which, from the permanent nature of their duties, should be Standing Committees : —

First, Committees of Arts.
Second, Committee on the Museum.
Third, Committee on the School of Industrial Science.
Fourth, Committee on Publications.

The Committees of Arts, designed to form in a large measure the working power of the Institute, should be arranged, when convenient, in conformity with the leading departments of the Museum, when this shall have been established; aiding the Curators with their counsels, and attending to the general interests of their several divisions.

It would be the duty of these Committees, by correspondence or otherwise, to aim at increasing the treasures of the Museum, and to unite with the Curators in stated Reports on the condition and progress of the respective departments. They should, moreover, be charged with the consideration of all questions and interests relating to the several branches which may be brought to the notice of the Institute, and be empowered or required to report their conclusions and suggestions to the general meeting. It should also be their province to propose subjects for investigation in their respective departments, to recommend experiments and trials of processes and machinery, and to designate such inventions or improvements as may be deemed worthy of special commendation or honorary reward.

From the great diversity of subjects comprised in the plan of the Institute, it would be necessary to group them under general heads; appointing a Committee only to each group, and looking to a division of these duties as the operations of the Institute and the progress of the Museum should demand. In this view, the following Committees of Arts may be designated as a suitable arrangement in the commencement of the undertaking: —

Standing Committees of Arts.

1. *On Mineral Materials.*

This Committee would have charge of whatever relates to the various rocks, sands, clays, marbles, and other mineral substances used in building and sculpture; the ores of iron, copper, lead, and other important metals; the metals themselves, in their crude or unwrought condition; the different kinds of coal; and, in fact, all the mineral substances employed in the useful arts, as well as what pertains to mining, quarrying, and the smelting of ores.

2. *On Organic Materials.*

This would embrace whatever is practically interesting in relation to the vegetable and animal substances used in the manufacturing and other arts, — as cotton, flax, hemp, wool, silk, hair, skins, furs, feathers, woods, barks, gums, dye-stuffs, oils, waxes, ivory, bone, shell, &c.; having in view their vegetable or animal sources, their culture and collection, their commercial importance, and their respective qualities in each variety as connected with the manufactured products.

3. *On Tools and Instruments.*

To this Committee would be intrusted the subjects of cutlery, and mechanics' tools of every variety, agricultural and horticultural implements, utensils of copper, tin, zinc, &c.; guns and weapons generally; surgical instruments; mathematical, chemical, and philosophical implements and apparatus, and instruments of music and horology; keeping in view the processes of manufacture, and special applications and uses of each.

4. *On Machinery and Motive Powers.*

The province of this Committee would embrace the construction and application of machinery in general, as applied to textile manufactures; to grinding, rolling, hammering, planing, pressing, sewing, and other mechanical efforts; to agricultural operations and to locomotion; together with all questions relating to the application of motive powers, and to the measurement of their efficiency.

5. *On Textile Manufactures.*

On this Committee would devolve all questions relating to the qualities, modes of production, and commercial value, of the various textile fabrics of cotton, wool, flax, hemp, silk, fur, hair, straw, &c., whether simple or mixed, woven, felted, or wrought by hand, as well as to the processes of dyeing, printing, and other ornamentation applied to them.

6. *On Manufactures of Wood, Leather, Paper, India Rubber, &c.*

This Committee would have charge of whatever relates to the various kinds of wooden-ware, cabinet-work, common and patent leather, oil-cloths, compositions for roofing, paper and paper-hangings, papier-mâché, japan-ware, book-binding, and the various fabrics of India rubber, gutta-percha, whalebone, ivory, straw, &c.; having, in each case, reference to the implements and processes of manufacture.

7. *On Manufactures of Pottery, Glass, and Precious Metals.*

To this would be referred all the processes and products of the Ceramic Arts, including the manufacture of porcelain, parian, earthen and stone wares, tiles and bricks; also whatever belongs to the composition and manufacture of the various descriptions of Glass, clear and colored, blown and cast, plain, pressed, engraved and cut. The same Committee would have charge of the fabrics in the precious stones, and in gold, silver, platinum, and aluminum; and of the methods and products of the arts of bronzing, silvering, and gilding, including the operations of electrotyping.

8. *On Chemical Products and Processes.*

The Committee in this department would give its attention to the entire range of chemical manufactures, including the production of what are technically called "chemicals;" as soda-ash, sulphuric and other acids, alum, copperas, saltpetre, Epsom and Glauber salts, Prussian blue, quinine, &c.; together with soaps, perfumery, stearine and burning fluids; also to the processes and products of fermentation and distillation; to the manufacture of starch, farina, cocoa, sugar, common salt; to that of gunpowder and other explosive mixtures; and to that of composts and artificial manures.

9. *On Household Economy, including Warming, Illumination, Water-supply, Ventilation, and the Preparation and Preservation of Food.*

On this Committee would devolve whatever relates to the construction and use of furnaces, stoves, steam and water apparatus, flues and other arrangements for the production and distribution of heat; the supply of gas, or other sources of illumination; the conveyance and delivery of water in streets and buildings; the means of securing ventilation in buildings, mines, and on shipboard; the improvements in culinary apparatus and processes; the various inventions for the preservation of food; and, in a word, the mechanical and chemical arrangements generally, appertaining to improved household economy, and to the protection of the public health.

10. *On Engineering and Architecture.*

To this Committee would be referred all questions relating to the qualities and applicability of the materials used in buildings or other structures; the survey, location, and construction of railroads, canals, bridges, reservoirs, aqueducts, paved avenues, and tunnels; the arrangement and decoration of open squares; the planning and erection of dwelling-houses, and of buildings for commercial, manufacturing, and educational or other public purposes; and, in a word, all the diversified works which come within the province of the architect and civil engineer; together with the no less important subjects of the modelling and construction of vessels, and the science and art of *naval architecture* in general.

11. *On Commerce, Navigation, and Inland Transport.*

This Committee would devote its attention to subjects and questions of a directly commercial character; taking cognizance of the staple products of different countries, their several varieties and adaptations, sources and commercial history; noting the statistics of foreign and domestic trade, and investigating the suggestions or the enterprises which tend to the enlargement of existing branches of commerce, or the creation of new ones. It would, moreover, give consideration to the various means of maritime and inland transport; to improvements in the model, rig, and propelling power of vessels; the amelioration of harbors; the construction of docks, piers, and other arrangements, for the security and convenience of shipping; and to the location and efficiency of railroads, and other channels of inland intercourse; keeping chiefly in view the economical questions of trade and exchange, which give these works of mechanical and engineering skill their high commercial importance.

12. *On the Graphic and Fine Arts.*

This Committee would take charge of all matters relating to the arts of drawing, designing, and making patterns; modelling, engraving, wood-cutting, printing, and photography, — regard being had to processes and implements, as well as to results; and, as the plan and collections of the Institute became enlarged, giving such attention to subjects of *higher art* as might contribute to the efficient, practical instruction which it is the aim of the Institute to secure.

Of the other Standing Committees previously suggested, the objects and duties might be briefly as follows: —

THE COMMITTEE OF THE MUSEUM would be charged with a general supervision of the architectural arrangements, furniture, internal plans, and business concerns, of the Museum; assigning to the Curators their respective spaces or compartments, and advising with these officers in all important business details of their several subdivisions. They should, moreover, have general care of all the buildings and grounds of the Institute, and should act in concert with the Committee next named in matters relating to the planning, furnishing, and allotment of lecture-rooms, and to the application of these or other parts of the building to lectures or other uses not designated in the regular operations of the Institute.

The Committee of the School of Industrial Science should be invested with the general supervision of this department, both in its organization and business affairs; looking to the efficient equipment and conduct of the School of Design, and to the provision of courses of lectures and class-room teachings in the various branches of Practical Science and the Arts, and to the organization of chemical and other laboratories for instruction and practical research.

The Committee of Publication should have the general direction of the printing of the Proceedings and Memoirs of the Institute, and of the publication of the "Journal" when established; and should be empowered to advise with the Editor or Editors of the latter as to the selection of articles, and the general literary conduct of the work.

II. MUSEUM OF INDUSTRIAL ART AND SCIENCE, OR CONSERVATORY OF ARTS.

In organizing and conducting the Museum of the Institute, reference should be had rather to the extent of practical instruction to be derived from it than to the multitude of objects which it might embrace. Its several departments, therefore, should aim, in the first place, at forming a collection of objects of prominent importance, as illustrating the respective Arts, however common and familiar they might be; and at so arranging them as to exhibit their history as natural products, or devices of Art, their distinctive characters, and the successive changes wrought upon them by the application of science, or mechanical skill. As specimens of materials, workmanship, and machinery accumulated, care should be taken to preserve this method of arrangement, wherever practicable; and to accord a prominent place to what might be called the *typical objects* in each Department, however large the general mass of its collection.

Nor, in regard to any part of the Museum, should the great purpose of *instruction* be lost sight of in the multitudinous gathering of materials. A mere miscellaneous collection of objects, however vast, has little power to instruct, or even to incite to inquiry. The practical teaching and the real suggestiveness of a Museum is almost wholly dependent on the clear and rational arrangement of its parts, and the leading ideas which rule in their classification. We would therefore aim at having the Departments of our Museum well distinguished from each other, and the objects in each placed in their true connections, so as to display readily their nature or construction, and to facilitate their comparison with others of the same class.

As regards *the arrangement of the Museum in Departments*, it would be premature at present to frame any very definite plan. The several groups of subjects referred to in connection with the organization of the Standing Committees of Arts may suffice to suggest the leading subdivisions most likely to be adopted, as at once simple, convenient, and conducive to practical utility. Referring to these somewhat in the order previously announced, it may be useful, in the present connection, to advert to their proposed scope and arrangement, and to note more particularly the value of the practical teachings which they might be expected to impart.

Let us then consider, first, the division comprising Mineral Materials, with the processes and products appertaining to them.

Here would be displayed a methodized series of the granites, sandstones, limestones, marbles, soapstones, slates, and other rocky materials, used in Architecture ; of the clays, flints, felspars, sands, and other ingredients, used in the manufacture of the several varieties of earthenware, porcelain, and glass ; of the ores of iron, copper, lead, zinc, manganese, and other valuable metals ; and of the different descriptions of fossil fuel, in their several gradations, from the hardest anthracite to lignite, asphaltite, and peat. Along with these, and arranged in corresponding positions, we should see specimens of the dressed and polished building materials; samples of the refined and levigated clays and other materials, ready for the potter and glassmaker; and specimens of the metals, both in their crude condition (as first obtained from the ore) and in the purity to which they are brought by subsequent operations.

In the same department would be gathered pictures, sections, maps, and models, — setting forth the geological and topographical conditions under which these different mineral materials are found on or beneath the earth's surface, illustrating the methods by which they are mined and transported, and exemplifying the processes by which they are wrought into shape, or transformed and purified, so as to be available for the purposes of the Arts.

Such a series of typical specimens, drawings, models, and other illustrations, while conveying valuable information in a connected shape even to transient observers, and greatly facilitating the inquiries of the systematic, general student, could not fail to prove a valuable help to the architect, engineer, and practical geologist, as well as to those engaged in iron-making and the other branches of metallurgy, and in the glass and ceramic manufactures.

The Department of ORGANIC MATERIALS, following the same principle of arrangement, would exhibit, in orderly connection, the various crude products as they are derived from their vegetable or animal sources, with the several stages of modification or refinement which fit them for the purposes of textile or other manufacture; and, in fact, *the whole history of each leading object, from its origin to its appropriation by the more advanced industrial processes.*

Thus, in the division allotted to textile fibres, we should have brought before us a series of specimens or drawings of the plants from which cotton, flax, hemp, and other vegetable fibres, are derived; a suite of the fibres, in their crude and in their prepared condition; magnified drawings of their form and structure as seen under the microscope; and an array of the different varieties of each as produced in this and in other countries. Similar suites of specimens, aided occasionally by drawings, would illustrate the history of wool and silk, from their crude state to their ultimate preparation; and furnish the means of comparing the greatly diversified qualities which they present, as coming from different breeds and localities, and as suited to the several fabrics in which they are employed.

So, in another division of the Department, we would find a series of the woods employed in building, and in cabinet and ornamental work, or for the uses of the dyer, each in a form to exhibit both transverse and longitudinal sections, and in the smoothed or polished as well as in the rough condition; and accompanied, where practicable, by a representation of the plant or tree from which it is derived. And so, again, the oils, waxes, gums, horn, whalebone, India rubber, gutta-percha, indigo, and madder, as well as tea, coffee, cocoa, and other articles of food or medicine, would be made to reveal their origin, and the processes by which they are prepared for consumption, or extracted, and made available in the Arts.

Thus arranged in all its divisions, with a view to clear and substantial instruction, the Department of Organic Materials would claim a place among the most useful branches of the Museum, not only as offering valuable knowledge to the general inquirer, but as furnishing fruitful suggestions and powerful helps to the artisan, the manufacturer, and the merchant, in the practical conduct of their pursuits.

In the several Departments of the MANUFACTURING ARTS, the vast variety of fabrics and products, classified according to their materials, textures, and ornamentation, would of themselves constitute an interesting subject of practical study and comparison.

The productions of the loom, the lathe, the forge, the pottery, and the glass furnace, gathered from foreign countries as well as from the manufactories at home, would enable us clearly to apprehend our relations to other producers, whether in regard to the intrinsic quality of the product, or the skill displayed in its form and decoration; while, through the knowledge thus acquired, our artisans and manufacturers would be saved much unsuccessful experiment, and be guided to new styles of texture and ornament, and to improved and often new processes of production.

Applying, as in the preceding instances, the plan of a progressive illustration of the objects, we should have the history of each leading fabric set forth by a series of specimens, commencing with the material as prepared for manipulation, and extending through each step of its manufacture to the perfected product. Thus, in the Department of Textile Manufactures, a suite of such progressive and typical specimens would show the gradations, from the prepared fibre of cotton, wool, flax, or silk, through the several forms of yarn or thread to the more and more complex tissues into which it is woven or interlaced; while another series might illustrate the several steps of the process of dyeing, and the entire history of the changes by which the blank cloth is finally impressed with the variegated colors of the printed fabric.

So, in the Departments of Glass, Fictile, and Metallic Manufactures, those of wood, leather, paper, gum elastic, gutta-percha, and the more strictly Chemical Arts, besides the extensive collection of fabrics in their various perfected forms, illustrating the condition of these several branches of Industrial Art at home and abroad, there would be presented a series of specimens showing the stages of the manufacturing process under each general division, and marking the mechanical or chemical agencies employed in their elaboration.

Not less interesting and important would be the Departments embracing the various classes of IMPLEMENTS AND MACHINERY, — the tools of the workers in woods, metals, stones, and other resisting materials; agricultural implements; weighing, measuring, and lifting apparatus; musical instruments; apparatus for philosophical experiments; together with specimens and models of the different kinds of clock and watch work, and of the endless forms of machinery employed in spinning, weaving, felting, sawing, planing, grinding, hammering, pressing, pumping, blowing, and other applications of mechanical energy to industrial uses. Added to these would be sections and other analytical representations of the more complex forms of machinery, to assist the general observer in comprehending their structure and essential connections, and to help the more critical student in his comparisons and improvements; while the practical interest of this division of the Museum would be yet further enhanced by the occasional *exhibition of new inventions* (whether of mechanism or of motive power), and by the display of particular classes of machinery in actual *working operation.*

Turning, lastly, to the Departments devoted to DOMESTIC AND GENERAL ARCHITECTURE, SHIP-BUILDING, INLAND TRANSPORT, and the various subjects of heating, illumination, water-supply, and ventilation, we should find in their collected illustrations rich sources of general and professional instruction. The models and drawings of buildings of various kinds; of sailing and steam vessels; of marine engines and propellers; of locomotives, cars, and other vehicles; of railway arrangements and electric telegraphs; and of the diversified mechanical and chemical contrivances employed in the supply and distribution of heat and light, water and air,—would be consulted with interest by the general student, at the same time that they offered to the architect, ship-builder, and engineer large opportunities for comparison, and precious helps and incentives to improvement. And, in the same connection, benefits of no small social importance might be anticipated from an ample illustration of the arrangements and inventions adapted to the economy of the household, and especially to the promotion of cleanliness, comfort, and health, in the workshops and in the homes of the poor.

In carrying on the Museum, whatever plan of subdivision may be adopted, it will be necessary to provide for each Department, as it becomes organized, a Superintending Officer, or Curator, whose duty it shall be to take charge of its collections; to attend to their arrangement and preservation; and to promote as much as possible the practical usefulness of his Department, by facilitating the inquiries of those who frequent it for instruction, as well as by laboring to enlarge its suites of illustrative objects. In all important changes and pecuniary concerns of the Department, the Curator should advise with the Committee of the Museum and the Committees of Arts interested in the subject; and they should be required to furnish an Annual Report of the condition and progress of the Department under their charge.

As permanency of office is essential to the efficient discharge of such duties, it is desirable to make the appointment of the Curators renewable as long as the Institute might desire. As, moreover, the labors and responsibilities of a fully organized department might be expected to occupy much of the time and interest of the Superintendent, we would deem it indispensable to attach to the curatorship, in each case, a suitable stated compensation, to be determined or modified according to the extent and changes of the several divisions of which the Curators have charge.

Such is an imperfect sketch of the Museum of Industrial Science and Art, which we would desire to see established as the central feature of our proposed Institute of Technology.

In framing its general plan, we have not hesitated to embrace the largest conceptions which the comprehensive nature of its objects and its prospective enlargement could suggest. We know, that, even under the happy auspices which seem to be gathering around our enterprise, the early development of the Museum must fall very far short of the imposing organization which our anticipations have traced; but it is the nature of such a plan to be susceptible of indefinite expansion. If we cannot begin with a long list of Departments and their attached Committees and Curators, we may group our first gatherings of Industrial Science and Art under larger and fewer subdivisions, and open our Museum with a smaller official staff, sure that its augmenting treasures will soon claim for it an organization far ampler and more complete.

Arranged and conducted according to the views which we have endeavored to set forth, we cannot doubt that it would acquire a practical value, even in its earlier stages, far beyond the measure of its extent,—a value as various and general as the interests and occupations illustrated by its collections; and commanding the hearty appreciation, not only of those immediately devoted to industrial pursuits, but of our intelligent fellow-citizens in every walk of life.

III. SCHOOL OF INDUSTRIAL SCIENCE AND ART.

In sketching thus far the plan and purposes of the proposed Institute of Technology, we have confined our view to the organization of a Society of Arts and an Industrial Museum; offering, at the same time, illustrations of the practical benefits to be anticipated from each. But our outline is not yet complete: these institutions—however beneficent in their respective spheres, as instruments for diffusing practical knowledge, and affording incentives and suggestions tending to the improvement of the industrial arts—could, of themselves, only in part fulfil the educational purposes which it should be the aim of the Institute to secure.

The productive talent of the community, as measured by its proficiency in the practical arts, requires for its steady and rapid development other helps than can be offered by the treasures of a Museum, or the discussions and publications of a Society. While it would, doubtless, profit largely by the opportunities for instruction which collections and publications can afford, it demands yet more urgently that *systematic training in the applied sciences,* which can alone give to the industrial classes a sure mastery over the materials and processes with which they are concerned.

Such a training, forming what may be called the intellectual element of production, has, we believe, become indispensable to fit us for successful competition with other nations in the race of industrial activity, in which we are so deeply interested. In the communities abroad, where manufactures and the mechanic arts have attained the greatest proficiency, and are now making the most rapid advances, such an education in practical science is recognized as the chief instrument in their extension and improvement; and the Schools of Practical Science, and the Polytechnic Institutes, designed to form an industrial class thus thoroughly trained in the principles of their respective arts, are highly honored, as well as liberally, and even munificently, endowed.

Fortunately, in this community, the education of the public schools is so general, and of so high a grade, that a good proportion of those who are destined for industrial pursuits are already well prepared to profit by the teachings and exercises of a School of Scientifie Technology. Indeed, considering our acknowledged superiority in this respect as compared with other nations generally, and having in view the eminently practical nature of the intellectual training incident to our social and political organization as a people, it can hardly be questioned that we are in a most favorable condition for attaining excellence in the pursuit of the practical sciences, and for reaping the highest advantages from their application in the wide fields of commerce, agriculture, and the mechanic and manufacturing arts.

It would seem, therefore, eminently expedient, in the organization of the Institute, to make provision for a Department to be called a *School of Industrial Science and Art,* in which regular courses of instruction should be given, by lectures and other teachings, in the various branches of the applied sciences and the arts; and where persons destined for any of the industrial pursuits might, at small expense, secure such training and instruction as would enable them to bring to their profession the increased efficiency due to enlarged views and a sure knowledge of fundamental principles, together with adequate practice in observation and experiment, and in the delineation of objects, processes, and machinery.

Without attempting, at present, to frame a very definite organization for this branch of the Institute, but looking rather to its practical recognition, in the beginning, as an integral part of our plan, however imperfectly carried out, we would mention certain departments of instruction, which we think could be advantageously established, even in the commencement of our enterprise. Among these, the first would be a —

School of Design.

This Department, looking chiefly to industrial uses, would aim to prepare its pupils for efficient service in the ornamental branches of manufactures, as well as in the pursuits of the mechanician, architect, and engineer; at the same time laying so broad a foundation of instruction, as to be a valuable help to general education, and to the higher culture of the Fine Arts. It should, therefore, be equipped with all the means for effective instruction, not only in geometrical, architectural, and free drawing, and the delineation of the apparatus and machinery of the arts, but in the copying and designing of figures and patterns for textile and other fabrics; in the making of patterns and models for fictile and metallic wares; in the principles regulating the arrangement and combination of colors, applied to these and other products; and in the scientific basis and leading operations of the arts of engraving and photography.

Such a practical training in the appropriate branches of drawing and design is of obvious necessity in the pursuits of the engineer, architect, and machinist; and we need hardly add, that, in many of the manufacturing arts, it has now become equally indispensable. The advance of social refinement is continually creating a demand for more artistic forms and coloring in the products of manufacturing skill, as well as for ever-successive novelties in their figure and decoration. Thus a wide field is opened for the exercise of taste, invention, and artistic ability, in the preparation of patterns for textile fabrics, for glass and pottery, and articles of household furniture; and, in the competition thus arising for new and tasteful devices, the prosperous pursuit of these departments of industry is often largely dependent on the extent of art-culture which can be brought to bear on what may be termed the æsthetic branch of the manufacture.

School of Mathematics.

Of the more strictly scientific part of the proposed School of Industrial Science and Art, a Department of *Elementary and Applied Mathematics* has especial claims to our attention, as relating to studies of fundamental importance in nearly every branch of the constructive and manufacturing arts. The teachings of this Department, without embracing the earliest rudiments of mathematics, would require — for the first few years at least — to be adapted to a humble grade of preliminary attainment. Besides common geometry, algebra, trigonometry, and descriptive and analytical geometry, they might, perhaps, include the elements of the differential and integral calculus. They should, however, dwell most especially on the application of the several subjects; in mensuration, surveying, navigation, map-making, and perspective; in computing the proportions of machinery, the form and strength of constructions, the value of mechanical forces; and in the innumerable other problems of a mathematical nature, which the mechanic, engineer, architect, and manufacturer may be called upon to resolve.

School of Physics.

Another leading department in the School of Industrial Science would be that of *General and Applied Physics,* — embracing the principles of mechanical philosophy, as relates to solids, liquids, and airs; the laws of heat, light, electricity, and magnetism; and the applications of these principles and laws, in the machinery, instruments, and processes of the manufacturing and mechanic arts. Under the latter heads, it would be the design to teach the relative properties and value of the different materials used in construction, and the principles regulating the distribution of tension and resistance among them; to illustrate the practical application of steam, heated air, water, the atmosphere, gravity, and other motive forces, together with the methods of determining their mechanical efficiency; and to explain the construction and working action of the various descriptions of machinery and engines to which these forces are applied: reference being made, throughout, to such of the machines, models, and drawings, contained in the Museum of the Institute, as might best answer the purposes of illustration.

In this division, it should be the first object to impart a thorough knowledge of the fundamental principles of the several branches of physics, as mathematically and experimentally demonstrated; and then to conduct the more strictly practical instruction, as much as possible, under the guidance of these primary truths. The mathematical treatment of the respective topics would of necessity be limited to the simpler lines of investigation. Yet it cannot be doubted, that even this elementary training in exact methods would be of great practical advantage to the inquirer, not only from the secure grasp of principles which it would confer, but from the habit of close observation and reasoning which it would enable him to apply in the practical questions of his profession.

School of Chemistry.

The subject of *Applied Chemistry* would also claim an important place in the plan of instruction here proposed. In this, as in the preceding departments of the School, the general doctrines and laws of chemical re-actions should be made to precede the study of the practical and industrial branches of the subject. The former might be taught by the demonstrations of the lecture-room: the latter could not be prosecuted in a manner to be practically available without personal training in analysis and experiment, and would therefore demand the facilities of an ample and well-appointed *Laboratory*. This we should hope to see early connected with the School of Industrial Science, and so equipped with the implements of practical chemistry as not only to provide for the ordinary exercises in analysis, but for the examination of soils, manures, and organic products, and for the illustration and study of the leading processes in dyeing, tanning, metallurgy, and the numerous other arts in which chemical re-actions are concerned.

School of Geology.

Lastly, to complete the circle of instruction essential to the plan of industrial education here contemplated, provision should be made for systematic teachings in *Physical Geology and Mining*, with so much of the general science as is important to illustrate the more practical branches of the subject. With the aid of maps, sections, and specimens, it would be the aim of this Department to teach whatever is known of the laws of succession of rock-formations, and of the various faults, flexures, and other disturbances or modifications, by which they are affected; and to point out more especially the geological structure and mineral characteristics of each of the great divisions of our own and the neighboring territories, the position and extent of the coal-fields, the belts of iron-bearing and other metalliferous rocks, and the geological relations and ranges of the various granites, sandstones, slates, soapstones, limestones, marbles, marls, clays, and other mineral aggregates, which have been found available for building or other purposes, or which may hereafter be brought into profitable use.

In this connection, the method of conducting geological and mineral surveys would be brought under view. The student would be taught whatever relates to the opening and extension of quarries, shafts, tunnels and drifts, and other details of mine-work, and to the winning, raising, and purification of the crude product; together with the drainage, ventilation, under-ground planning, and entire economy, of the mine: while, by the systematic study of specimens, he would be instructed in the characteristic appearances and properties of the more useful building-rocks, ores, coals, and other mineral materials; and would be prepared to test and estimate their value as applied to particular uses, and to make a proper selection, where necessary, between the similar products of different quarries, deposits, or mines.

Thus various in its practical instructions, both as regards principles and details, this Department of the School of Applied Science would not only offer facilities for professional training to those engaging in the pursuit of practical geology and mining, but, by innumerable facts and suggestions, would render most important service in agriculture, architecture, engineering, and most of the industrial arts.

Such is an imperfect sketch of the Departments of instruction which we would consider most essential in the strictly educational branch of the Institute. In conducting them, it would be the object to provide substantial and continuous courses of teaching, such as, while imparting a knowledge of the principles, facts, and processes connected with the Arts, should cultivate the habits of observation and exact thought, which are so conducive to the progress of invention and the development of intelligent industry.

In some of these Departments, — as drawing, operative chemistry, and mathematics, — the instructions would of necessity be chiefly conducted by *class-studies* and *recitations*, and *laboratory exercises*, requiring little or no aid from formal lectures; while, in others, — such as physics, general chemistry, and geology, — the plan of *lecture-room teaching* could be advantageously and habitually employed.

In arranging the plan and courses of instruction, provision would be made for the two classes of persons for whose benefit they are designed, — those who enter the school with the view of a progressive systematic training in applied science, and who have the preliminary knowledge, as well as time, for a continuous prosecution of its studies; and the far more numerous class, who may be expected to resort to its lecture-rooms for such useful knowledge of scientific principles as they can acquire without methodical study, and in hours not occupied by active labor.

The former would of necessity be subjected to classification and direction in their studies, as well as examinations and other tests of acquirement in the progress and at the close of their terms. The latter, without having access to the exercises of the classroom, would be admitted to the courses of lectures on general and applied science, subject only to the conditions and restraints that are usual in public lectures generally. To neither class would we propose to offer gratuitous instruction; but we would hope, that, through the prospering resources of the Institute, the entire systematic training of the school might be placed within reach of aspiring students of humble means, and that the lecture-room instructions might be made accessible to all at only an inconsiderable expense.

In regard to the latter feature of the School, we may remark, that, as the system of merely popular lecturing in its usual form would be inconsistent with the grave practical purposes which we have in view, it could not be recognized in connection with our plan. We would, however, anticipate much valuable aid from courses of lectures on subjects not directly provided for in the School, but of a nature to be conducive to the general objects of the Institute. Such would be the history of commerce, manufactures, and the mechanic arts; biographies of eminent inventors, and other benefactors of industry; important questions in political economy and trade; the principles of architecture, painting, sculpture, and of fine-art criticism, and illustrations of special inventions and discoveries in general and industrial science; and, for these additions to the educational advantages of the Institute, we might confidently rely on the assistance of the members and other friends qualified to advance its purposes in connection with industrial and general education.

In the features of the plan here sketched, it will be apparent that the education which we seek to provide, although eminently practical in its aims, has no affinity with that instruction in mere *empirical routine* which has sometimes been vaunted as the proper education for the industrial classes. We believe, on the contrary, that the most truly practical education, even in an industrial point of view, is one founded on a thorough knowledge of scientific laws and principles, and which unites with habits of close observation and exact reasoning a large general cultivation. We believe that the highest grade of scientific culture would not be too high as a preparation for the labors of the mechanic and manufacturer; and we read in the history of social progress ample proofs that the abstract studies and researches of the philosopher are often the most beneficent sources of practical discovery and improvement.

But such complete and comprehensive training can, in the nature of things, be accessible to only comparatively few; while the limited and special education which our plan proposes, would, we hope, fall within the reach of a large number whom the scantiness of time, means, and opportunity, would exclude from the great seats of classical and scientific education in the Commonwealth.

It will thus be seen, from the peculiar character and objects of this Department of the Institute, that it could not interfere with the interests of the established schools of learning devoted to general literary and scientific education. Aiming to supply the industrial classes with a knowledge and training of which they are specially in need, and which it would be incompatible with the purpose and organization of the universities and colleges to attempt to provide, it would, we feel assured, command the good wishes and active sympathies of the scholars, and men of science, who dispense the high instruction of these schools. Nor can we doubt that it would be gladly welcomed by all those who are practically occupied in the Arts, as a new source of success and enjoyment in their labors ; while, by the large-minded manufacturers, merchants, mechanics, and agriculturists, who control the material fortunes of the Commonwealth, it would be heartily and liberally recognized as a needed and truly momentous addition to our means of industrial as well as of educational prosperity.

WILLIAM B. ROGERS, *Chairman.*

MARSHALL P. WILDER,	DR. S. CABOT, Jun.,
SAMUEL H. GOOKIN,	G. W. PRATT,
M. D. ROSS,	AMOS BINNEY,
B. S. ROTCH,	DR. S. KNEELAND, Jun.,
R. C. WATERSTON,	CHARLES L. FLINT,
ALFRED ORDWAY,	J. D. PHILBRICK,
ALEX. H. RICE,	GEO. B. EMERSON,
E. S. TOBEY,	ERASTUS B. BIGELOW,
JAMES M. BEEBE,	CHARLES H. DALTON,

Committee.

At a meeting of gentlemen interested in the establishment of an Institute of Technology, held at the rooms of the Board of Trade, at 11, A. M., Oct. 5, the foregoing plan was read by Professor ROGERS ; and, on vote, was approved, and its publication recommended.

www.ingramcontent.com/pod-product-compliance
Lightning Source LLC
LaVergne TN
LVHW011125110826
845150LV00008B/2255

* 9 7 8 1 4 1 8 1 9 5 5 7 1 *